MANCHESTER AIRPORT 75
1938 – 2013

Written and researched by Mark Williams

Published by RINGWAY PUBLICATIONS
www.ringwaypublications.com

Ringway Publications

First published in Great Britain 2013

A catalogue record of this book is available from the British Library

ISBN No: 978-0-9570826-3-2

Printed and bound in Great Britain by

Beamreach (UK) Ltd
22 Pepper Street
Lymm
Cheshire
WA13 OJB
www.beamreachuk.co.uk

CONTENTS

PHOTOGRAPH CREDITS

Front Cover:
October 22nd 2009. Old meets new! Air France Airbus A.320-211 F-GFKJ and KLM Boeing 737-8K2 PH-BXA are seen parked together, sporting retro liveries.
(Nik French)

Back Cover:
November 1960. The new Control Tower is essentially finished, even to the point where the 'MANCHESTER' lettering has been completed, although the terrace infrastructure and more importantly, the brand new terminal, are still quite a way off completion. The new terminal, two piers and spectator terraces were finally opened by HRH Duke of Edinburgh on October 22nd 1962.
(MIA Archive Collection)

ACKNOWLEDGEMENTS

I would like to thank everyone who has contributed by supplying photographs, data, documents and information.

My eternal gratitude goes out to the following:

PHOTOGRAPH CREDITS
Geoff Ball, Ian Barrie, Lee Collins, Mark Duffy, Nik French, Andy Hall, Peter Hampson, Dave Jones, Alan Jones, MIA Archive Collection, Denis Norman, Michael Oldham, Hubert Parrish, Stuart Prince, Paul Rowland, Terry Shone, Barry Swann, Michael Wait, Rick Ward and Mark White.

PROOF-READER
Martin Dennett.

MANCHESTER AIRPORT ARCHIVE
Michael Hancock, Business Records Officer.

MANCHESTER CENTRAL LIBRARY
The Local Studies Department for arranging access to their archives for the last twenty-five years.

RESEARCH/MOVEMENTS
To everyone who helped fill any gaps in my research, with special thanks to Ian Barrie, John Duffield (movements) and Chris Walkden (movement logs). Also The Aviation Society (Winged Words for reference) Air-Britain and magazines for reference by the Cheshire Aviation Society, Air-Britain and North West Air News.

Mark Williams

RINGWAY PUBLICATIONS

BOOKS:

SEVENTIES RINGWAY
EIGHTIES RINGWAY 1980-1984
EIGHTIES RINGWAY 1985-1989
WOODFORD IN PICTURES

Forthcoming:
Diversion Days – The 1970s
Sixties in Pictures Vol I & II
Football Comes to Manchester Airport 1990-1999
Football Comes to Manchester Airport 2000-2010
Nineties Ringway Vol I & II
The Hubert Parrish Photographic Collection

MANCHESTER MOVEMENTS CDs

Sixties Movements
Seventies Movements
Eighties Movements
Nineties Movements
50 Years of Diversions 1960-2010

Forthcoming:
Noughties Movements

Visit our historic website:
www.ringwaypublications.com

We can be contacted through our website or by emailing:
info@ringwaypublications.com

INTRODUCTION

Once the initial fanfare of the airport's opening on June 25th 1938 had died down, scepticism started to form, particularly within the local media. The Manchester Guardian reported on Saturday August 20th 1938 that business errands accounted for the majority of air travellers using Manchester-Ringway. Destinations such as the Isle of Man and Northern Ireland were proving popular and there was also a 'trickle of traffic' between Manchester and London.

However, there was also a note of negativity towards this new trend for air travel when they reported they had sufficient grounds to believe that unless the travelling time was substantially reduced, no real improvement in the passenger figures could be expected. As an example the flying time of 2¼ hours between Manchester and London plus the travelling time between the two cities produced a total journey time confirming the claim by the London, Midland and Scottish Railway 'that its quicker by rail'.

When World War II broke out a year later in 1939, this became academic. During the war Manchester-Ringway played a vital part in providing a home for 613 Squadron and being used for the test flights of more than 4,500 warplanes produced by A.V.Roe, Fairey Aviation and others.

The airports seventy-five year history is long and complex and has been left for others to discuss. This publication is an attempt to capture the atmosphere of Manchester-Ringway by means of the photographs within. Many types of aircraft and airlines which have come and gone are featured as are the development of facilities such as new terminals, its own railway station and a brand new second runway.

The routes served from Manchester, which are also shown, all helped towards the making of today's Manchester Airport, now handling in more than 19 million passengers per year.

Mark Williams

July 1938. The completed hangar, control tower and terminal are seen a few months after opening. The apron had limited hard-standing and a spectator area is above the terminal. A fire engine and ambulance are located inside the outbuilding to the right. The letter 'C' on the tower denotes the international sign for pilots to report after landing. *(MIA Archive Collection)*

August 12th 1938. KLM Lockheed 14 PH-ASL 'Lepelaaf' is pictured two months after the airport's opening, with Alderman Tom Regan and members of the Gorton Labour party. Tom Regan was a founder member of the Airport Special Committee in 1928, Chairman from 1949 to 1951 and a committee member until 1974. Initially KLM used Douglas DC-2 aircraft for their Amsterdam services but changed to the 11-seat Lockheed following insufficient passenger loads. *(MIA Archive Collection)*

June 1949. Danny Kaye is seen arriving onboard Scottish Aviation DC-3 G-AGZG ahead of his appearance at the Palace Theatre, Manchester. *(MIA Archive Collection)*

June 1951. Members of the Women's Auxiliary Air Force awaiting air experience flights in Airspeed Oxford W6642, which had recently arrived from RAF Brawdy. The aircraft made four flights before returning to Brawdy. *(Hubert Parrish)*

April 13th 1952. Airviews Auster J1N Alpha and Dragon Rapide G-AGXN await their next series of pleasure flights during the Easter weekend. *(Hubert Parrish)*

May 7th 1954. BOAC Stratocruiser G-ALSC is seen departing off Runway 24 on its inaugural flight to New York via Prestwick as BA525, but the service only lasted until November. BOAC returned in April 1957, this time operating Douglas DC-7s and by November the schedules were three times weekly to New York and four times weekly to Montreal, but again it terminated by December due to main runway work. 1958 saw the return of BOAC Douglas DC-7s and by 1959 the Bristol Britannia had been introduced, with G-AOVE operating the New York service. *(Hubert Parrish)*

June 29th 1959. USAF C-124 Globemaster 20956 is also departing Runway off 24. This was one of many USAF transport aircraft to visit during the year, collecting various supplies from RAF Burtonwood when it was winding down. However, in 1963 the American Air Force announced their intention to reactivate the World War Two base. *(Hubert Parrish)*

September 1959. The Airport Control room is seen with the Fairey complex visible in the background. At the time Manchester Airport had three active runways, with 06/24 acting as the main runway for most arrivals/departures, 10/28 for light aircraft and 02/20 which ran parallel with the Fairey hangars was mainly used for their purposes. *(MIA Archive Collection)*

November 22nd 1960. Interocean Airways Douglas DC-4 LX-IAL arrived on diversion the previous afternoon whilst en route from Belfast to Birmingham. *(MIA Archive Collection)*

June 2nd 1961. Air France SE.210 Caravelle F-BHRD has just arrived on the first of the airline's new daily service to Paris. Air France had ceased schedules to Manchester during 1954 due to lack of aircraft. The SE.210 Caravelle was also the first jet airliner to land at Manchester, when F-BHHI touched down on a demonstration flight on the 30th July 1958. *(Hubert Parrish)*

1961. Against the backdrop of the Airport Hotel which is still in existence today, Air Safari Hermes G-ALDT is seen wearing Skyways colours on very short finals. *(MIA Archive Collection)*

July 12ʰ 1961. BEA Viscount G-AOYN arrived on a specially chartered flight from Heathrow with an unusual passenger, Russian cosmonaut Yuri Gagarin, the first man in space. The visit had been arranged at the request of the Amalgamated Union of Foundry Workers, one of the world's largest unions and to everyone's surprise the invitation was accepted by the Soviets. The visit of Major Yuri Gagarin which took place exactly three months after his historic space flight was only the second stop outside the Soviet Bloc on what became a very long world tour. Gagarin had just visited Finland before continuing on to many other countries. In contrast to some of his later visits, which concentrated on meeting Heads of State and Presidents, his visit to Manchester was deliberately organised to create a sense of solidarity between the workers of England and the Soviet Union. Thousands of expectant people turned out in the pouring rain to welcome the cosmonaut. It was Gagarin's first flight in a British plane and for a short time he took over the controls on the way to Manchester. A huge crowd had pushed their way through the airport gates and onto the tarmac to greet Gagarin as he stepped from the plane. A surge from the crowd carried him away from the party of officials waiting to meet him but eventually the police managed to force a path and guide Gagarin back to the jostled city representatives. Included was the Mayor of Stretford who was introduced to Gagarin, but he didn't get a chance to speak to him due to the cheering and applauding by the crowds. Gagarin then tried to make his way to a waiting car, but again he was swept up by the crowd, this time in a sea of backslapping to the far end of a hangar, well away from his car. Airport officials stated it was the biggest and most enthusiastic welcome ever given to anyone at the airport. Once safely in his car, he was driven to the union's Moss Side headquarters, through streets lined with cheering and waving crowds, despite the pouring rain. His next stop was the giant AEI works at Trafford Park, known as 'Metros' where thousands of workers mobbed him. Police had to stop the traffic and force back the crowds to allow his car through the gates. His welcome was tumultuous and Gagarin retained his composure and smiled throughout. His last engagement in the region was a civic banquet at Manchester Town Hall. Huge crowds lined his route again, which passed by Manchester United's football ground. The United players came out to cheer him and a train driver sounded his whistle in salute, to which Gagarin responded with a wave and a grin. At the Town Hall a crowd of more than six thousand people waiting to see him was the largest the police had seen. The Russian National Anthem was played and the red flag was raised over the Town Hall. As Gagarin saluted a small boy broke through the police cordon and shook the Mayor's hand. He took a quick photo of Gagarin and then stood staring at him. The Town Hall had only been given twenty-four hours notice of Gagarin's visit. At the luncheon, Sir Bernard Lovell was introduced to Gagarin and who thanked him for all the assistance Jodrell Bank had given the Soviet space programme in tracking their early launches. Sir Bernard hoped that Gagarin would have time to visit Jodrell Bank, but his schedule was too tight. After a whistle-stop round of engagements, he returned to the airport for his flight to London aboard Viscount G-AOYN where thousands of people were still waiting for him. As he reached the top of the steps leading on to the aeroplane he turned, grinned and blew a kiss to the crowds! *(MIA Archive Collection)*

June 2nd 1963. During the 1960s and well into the 1970s, IT flights were flown by Iberia aircraft on behalf of Aviaco. In 1960 the first of series of flights began when the airline operated a weekly flight to Palma with Convair CV-440s. By1963, Iberia L-1049Gs were being used, operating flight AO1118/9, also from/to Palma. The Constellation was used until 1965 with the newer Caravelles taking over the following year. The last Iberia Constellation L-1049G to visit was EC-AIO on the 2nd October 1965. *(MIA Archive Collection)*

August 31st 1963. KLM was the first International airline to fly scheduled services from Manchester upon its opening in 1938. During the 1960s, the Viscount dominated the route in the early-mid 1960s before the Lockheed Electra took over from around 1965 until their new Douglas DC-9 began to be delivered in 1967. *(Hubert Parrish)*

August 1965. BEA commenced jet services from Manchester on July 1st 1965 when Trident 1 G-ARPS departed at 0931 to inaugurate a six-times weekly service serving Paris-Le Bourget. It was carrying the Lord Mayor of Manchester and a party of VIPs amongst the passengers. The flight took just fifty minutes, shaving twenty five minutes off the schedule. *(MIA Archive Collection)*

April 27th 1966. The first Russian-designed aircraft to land at Ringway was the twin piston-engined Avia 14-32A, which was basically a Czech-built Ilyushin IL-14M. OK-BYU which is owned by the Czech Government arrived at 1451 from Glasgow and departed the following day for Heathrow. *(MIA Archive Collection)*

August 27th 1966. Due to strict IATA rules regarding transatlantic charters which were mainly in place to protect the main airlines, so-called affinity charters were popular during the 1960s. These were organised by groups as a cheaper alternative for individuals or families visiting relations in the USA and Canada. Here one such group are about to board Pan American Boeing 707-321B, ultimately bound for New York. *(MIA Archive Collections)*

1966. Bing Crosby and his wife are greeted on the tarmac at Manchester. *(MIA Archive Collection)*

July 25ᵗʰ 1967. Royal Canadian Air Force C-47 KP221, which had arrived the previous evening from Lahr, was assigned to the Canadian Joint Staff and based at Northolt. This Dakota was the personal mount of a 3-star General and displayed the 3-stars under the cockpit window. *(Geoff Ball)*

15

1967. This picture shows the four magnificent chandeliers, officially unveiled when Prince Philip opened the new terminal in October 1962. The chandeliers, each costing £3,000 and weighing 2 tonnes, were 17ft long and contained 1,300 pieces of crystal between them. They were designed by Royal architect Stefan Buzas, hand blown by glass maker Bruno Zanetti and manufactured by the famous Venini factory on the Venetian island of Murano, Italy. *(MIA Archive Collection)*

1968. At this time the 'MANCHESTER' letters were still worn on the outside of the tower, but had been removed by 1970. Also of note is the lack of spectators on the terrace, although there are several at the window of the terminal building. *(MIA Archive Collection)*

17

1968. The services provided for the departure travellers included a self-service cafeteria and a bar in the departure lounge. For the more discerning traveller, meals and cocktails were available in the more comfortable and relaxed atmosphere of the Lancaster Restaurant. *(MIA Archive Collection)*

July 2ⁿᵈ 1968. A very rare visitor to Manchester was JAT Douglas DC-3 YU-ACA. This aircraft arrived from Belgrade via Brussels with spares for fellow SE.210 Caravelle YU-AHB, which had gone tech on its arrival on an IT flight from Pula. *(Geoff Ball)*

October 12th 1968. Douglas DC-6 XC-DUC operated by the EBANO Oil Corporation had arrived from Marseilles to drop off computer parts, before departing for Shannon. It was later revealed that the aircraft was also carrying Alouettes XC-DUM & XC-DUN. *(Geoff Ball)*

1969. An interior view of the up-market Lancaster Restaurant situated at the end of the terminal. *(MIA Archive Collection)*

April 7th 1969. The departure to Beauvais of Channel Airways Viscount 810 G-AVHE, demonstrates how popular watching aircraft had become by the late 1960s. Note not only the vast crowds on the terraces but also the number of faces at the window of the terminal building! The fact that the Airport was such a popular place to go, particularly at weekends, was owed to the excellent spectator facilities at the time. *(Geoff Ball)*

May 14th 1969. Ringway played host to many military flights, such as Dassault MD315 Flamont No.301, one of the more unusual types operated by the French Air Force and not common to Manchester. It was operating a training flight en-route from Arbroath - Paris-Le Bourget. *(Geoff Ball)*

June 12th 1969. As part of the 50th Anniversary of the first non-stop transatlantic flight by Mancunian John Alcock and his Scottish co-pilot Arthur Whitten Brown, replica Vickers Vimy G-AWAU built at BAC Weybridge, was flown in to take part in the popular exhibition. However, on July 14th disaster struck as it was being readied for departure to Hucknall, when the suns ray ignited the canvas on the lower port wing. Luckily the Airport Fire Service contained the fire quickly and the aircraft was eventually rebuilt and displayed at the RAF Museum at Hendon.
(Above Geoff Ball, below MIA Archive Collection)

May 4ᵗʰ 1969. The Russian built Tupolev TU-134 made its debut at Manchester on this date. Yugoslav airline Aviogenex used two aircraft, YU-AHH & YU-AHI during that year, which were original TU-134s with the glass nose. Operating to Pula, Dubrovnik and Split, they were soon replaced with TU-134As (without the glass nose) which served the airline until 1988 when they were replaced by Boeing 727s. *(MIA Archive Collection)*

June 22ⁿᵈ 1969. A photographic account of the chaos on a busy summer's Sunday, due to be swept away in 1972 when work commenced on the extension of the new terminal, the third pier and the multi-storey car park. *(MIA Archive Collection)*

July 22nd 1969. TIA Boeing 727-171C N1728T is seen taking a quiet moment before returning to New York. They only used the B.727 for transatlantic flights to Manchester twice. This was the first and both were in 1969. The larger Douglas DC-8s were more regularly used and by 1979/1980, flights were operated by their three Douglas DC-10s and three Boeing 747s. *(Geoff Ball)*

December 9th 1969. The arrival from Paris-Orly of L-1049C F-BGNG on a gloomy Tuesday morning marked the final visit of a Constellation to Manchester. The aircraft, operating an outbound freight charter to Bratislava, had been formerly operated by Air France initially as a passenger aircraft, but was later converted to a freighter. It was sold to French operator Catair in June 1968, but had been withdrawn from service by 1976. *(Dave Jones)*

August 17th 1970. BOAC B.747 G-AWNA arrived for a 75 minute VIP visit during a heavy thunderstorm. Strict security was enforced and only airport, airline staff and VIP guests were allowed onboard. It parked on Stand 28, the end gate of the International pier, where everyone had the opportunity to observe it from close quarters! The airline, which morphed into British Airways, would eventually introduce the type onto services from Manchester in 1977. *(Both MIA Archive Collection)*

January 5th 1971. This was the scene during the morning after receiving 52 weather diversions the day before due to dense, freezing fog affecting most of the UK, particularly Heathrow and Gatwick. These were on top of the 34 diversions which arrived on January 3rd. By the time of this photograph most of the 86 extra aircraft were still on the ground, double-parked on stands, parked on taxiways, disused runways and even the South Side, where the lighter side of aviation at Manchester resides. At one point during the afternoon of the 4th, Manchester was the only major airfield in the UK open and able to accept diversions. *(Dave Jones)*

October 3rd 1971. A total of 24 weather diversions arrived into Manchester, including five Boeing 747s. Four of these were on the ground at the same time and it was the first time that the type had diverted into Manchester. Their arrival aroused considerable curiosity from the general public and this shot of three of the aircraft shows Aer Lingus EI-ASJ (IN2140 from New York), N93102 (TW700 from New York) and N770PA (PA002 from New York). *(Dave Jones)*

November 22ⁿᵈ 1971. A very rare photograph shows the first visit of the unique Aerospatiale Super Guppy, F-BTGV. It was basically a converted Boeing 377 Stratocruiser, with up-rated engines. It was a frequent visitor to Manchester, along with three others, transporting Airbus wings for assembly at Toulouse, and later Bremen. The wings would be roaded in from the factory at Broughton, near Chester early on Sunday mornings to keep road disruption to a minimum. At the time the following saying was coined: 'Every Airbus is delivered by the wings of a Boeing!' *(Geoff Ball)*

May 22ⁿᵈ 1972. Bolivian Air Force Convair 340 TAM-43 was one of three aircraft on delivery to the Bolivian Air Force. One of the other aircraft, TAM-41 which was also acting as the radio ship, developed a problem, so all three diverted into Manchester. It's believed that the smoke problem in the cockpit was caused by an engineer leaving an oily rag in the exhaust! *(Peter Hampson)*

August 16th 1972. This is the first visit of the L.1011 Tristar to Manchester, when demonstrator N305EA 'Halcyon Days' arrived in the bright sunshine. Wearing basic Eastern Airlines and Court Line titles, it was on a demonstration flight from Luton, before departing to Amsterdam with various travel press and travel agency staff onboard. On arrival it came under the scrutiny of the local media and the spectators gathered on the end of Pier B. Looking radiant, the aircraft's cabin crew are seen posing for the photographers and onlookers. *(Above Geoff Ball, below MIA Archive Collection)*

November 23rd 1972. Five months after the debut of the L.1011, it was the turn of McDonnell Douglas to debut their new wide body, the DC-10. G-AZZC 'Eastern Belle', one of two ordered by Laker Airways, arrived from Gatwick on a demonstration flight to local travel agents before departing to Glasgow the next day for further flights. The airline began using the type from April 1973, operating a weekly charter from/to Toronto. *(MIA Archive Collection)*

1973. The Information Desk in the International Departures Terminal. *(MIA Archive Collection)*

March 27th 1973. Presumably this line-up of cabin crew in the native costumes of various countries was an indicator to the destinations the airline was intending to serve. *(MIA Archive Collection)*

April 3rd 1973. Aeromexico Douglas DC-8-51 XA-SIA is seen departing for Heathrow with the President of Mexico and his entourage onboard, following the first leg of his official state visit to Britain. He had arrived the previous evening on the same aircraft for an overnight stay in Manchester. This was his first visit and to date the only visit to Manchester by the Mexican-state airline. *(Dave Jones)*

April 25th 1973. Alitalia Boeing 747-238 I-DEMU arrived during the afternoon, bringing in Juventus fans for their European Cup tie with Derby County at the Baseball Ground later that evening. The game finished 0-0, but having already lost the first leg 3-1, it meant Derby was out of the tournament. *(Geoff Ball)*

March 25th 1974. The main phase of the 1970 Expansion Plan was officially opened on this date. It consisted of the Inter-continental Pier C, complete with telescopic air bridges and a new apron, a new multi-storey car park and extensions to the existing terminal. Ironically the first flight to use Pier C wasn't a Manchester flight, but instead it was Heathrow weather diversion Alia B.707 JY-ADP, arriving with King Hussain of Jordan onboard. *(MIA Archive Collection)*

May 5th 1974. One of the most colourful airlines to visit Manchester was Luton-based Court Line, owned by the Clarkson group. The airline had slowly built their operations during the early 1970s and by 1974 they had a BAC 1-11 based, which operated to various holiday destinations, but by May the economical storm clouds were gathering. The Clarkson group collapsed on August 15th 1974, leaving thousands of overseas holidaymakers stranded and many more without a summer holiday to look forward to. The final Court Line flight into Manchester on the day of the collapse was pink BAC 1-11 G-AXMF, operating as OU682 from Malta. *(Geoff Ball)*

March 5th 1975. Another wide-bodied first visit was the Airbus A.300, which debuted on this date. OO-TEF was operating a football charter bringing Anderlecht fans in for a European match with Leeds United. *(Peter Hampson)*

July 12ᵗʰ 1975. The Red Arrows, consisting of ten Folland Gnat T.1s, are seen in the South Bay having just arrived from RAF Cranwell. They departed the following afternoon to perform their spot in the Barton Air Show. Back up as always was provided by an RAF C130 Hercules, this time XV207. *(MIA Archive Collection)*

October 14ᵗʰ 1975. Although Fairey Aviation had virtually wound up its major aviation activities at Manchester during the 1960s, activity increased from 1974 onwards when the company began exporting its portable bridges overseas. Tradewinds/IAS Canadair CL-44 G-BCWJ is seen here on one such operation. The Fairey Group went into receivership in 1977 and their last remaining hangar was consigned to history when it was demolished in 1982. *(MIA Archive Collection)*

October 21st 1975. There were many features within the main terminal that made it uniquely distinct. The four chandeliers, the airline boards that ran either side, the Infolux departures board, the magnificent view of the apron from the windows at the far end and the 'black-ribbed' tile floor with its own unusual sound when luggage trolleys passed over it! *(MIA Archive Collection)*

November 30th 1975. A foggy weekend across the UK causing travel chaos, particularly for air travellers, led to a busy weekend for Manchester Airport handling weather diversions. JAL Boeing 747-246B JA8122 is seen parked on Gate 23, having recently arrived from Tokyo via Copenhagen on the first visit by the Japanese airline. *(MIA Archive Collection)*

February 1st 1976. The mid-1970s saw an increasing amount of crew training flights at Manchester. Prior to their entry into service in 1975, British Airways extensively used Manchester and Prestwick for these flights. One aircraft could operate numerous flights during a single day with up to three different aircraft on some occasions. A new airline to the scene was Gulf Air, who had recently acquired the first of its four Tristar aircraft. L1011 G-BDCW is seen here on a brief stop at Manchester before setting off on its next mission! *(Geoff Ball)*

May 9th 1976. It's hard to believe nowadays that the Iranian Air Force ran a series of flights from Manchester, roughly once a month until September 1977. Boeing 707-3J9C 5-244 is seen having just arrived on the first of these flights. *(Geoff Ball)*

August 29th 1976. Although fog was not unusual during the summer, the sun tended to burn it away quickly, but on this occasion it affected Heathrow until well into the morning. Of the twenty-one arrivals into Manchester, eight were wide-bodied diversions. A number of these aircraft are parked on a main taxiway and this shot shows that apron space was definitely at premium! Despite handling its own summer holiday traffic, the airport still managed to operate normally. *(Geoff Ball)*

October 22nd 1976. McCulloch International Boeing 720-022 N7201U is seen arriving on a gloomy Sunday. It was the personal transport of Peter Frampton, one of the biggest superstars at the time. It had a VIP interior with a maximum capacity of forty passengers. The starboard side of fuselage carried the inscription "Gary Wright" and the port side read "Frampton Comes Alive", referring to his multi-million selling live album. He'd arrived at Manchester for a concert that evening as part of his world tour. This aircraft also had the notoriety of being the first Boeing 720 ever produced. *(Geoff Ball)*

November 15th 1976. Concorde G-BOAA was the first to visit Manchester, touching down in the dark the previous night at 2108 as 'Speedbird Concorde 578 from Washington. The following day thousands of sightseers turned up to witness the aircraft parked on the end of the international pier. British Airways had introduced the type in January 1976 operating to Bahrain and later to Washington on May 24th 1976. *(MIA Archive Collection)*

December 21st 1976. Argosy 9Q-COA had arrived on October 12th 1976 as former-RAF example XR136. Work was carried at Dan-Air's recently opened maintenance facility, which up to this point had been mainly looking after its own aircraft. The aircraft had been purchased by Otrag Range Air Services, who planned to use two aircraft as support for the assembly of a missile launch facility in Zaire, which was in competition with NASA and the European rocket, Ariane. *(Geoff Ball)*

March 12th 1977. This colourful aircraft, Ted Smith Aerostar N300AM, aborted its attempt on a round-the-world speed record after developing technical trouble. It was a first visit of type, arriving en route Gander-Frankfurt after being forced to divert into Manchester with low oil pressure. It left after receiving two hours attention on the South Side. *(Geoff Ball)*

December 7th 1977. In 1971 when Balair ceased operating their Douglas DC-6s on their summer IT flights to Basle, it seemed unlikely that we'd see piston aircraft used on scheduled flights again, but in April 1977 Finnair began a weekly freighter service to Helsinki via Heathrow with their Douglas DC-6B swing-tail freighter, OH-KDA. This service eventually increased to thrice-weekly by 1981, but unfortunately Douglas DC-9Fs took over the route in October 1981. *(Geoff Ball)*

December 18th 1978. Swissair's operations into Heathrow were severely affected by fog, so they used Boeing 747-257 HB-IGB on Manchester's SR842 Zurich flight; with additional passengers for Heathrow who were subsequently transported to London by surface transport. *(Geoff Ball)*

June 4th 1978. When B-17 Flying Fortress G-BEDF touched down at Manchester prior to performing at the Barton Air Show, American movie star Elliott Gould also arrived as part of the crew. He spent around ninety minutes on the ground chatting with the ground crew. *(MIA Archive Collection)*

July 21ˢᵗ 1978. Air Malta were leasing two classic aircraft, owned and operated by Airtrust Singapore. Today's arrival of N48062 (KM780 from Malta) which had been anticipated for many weeks, was the first visit of a Convair CV-880. Seen here having just arrived on a warm Friday evening, it's still in basic Cathay Pacific colours. It was memorable for the smoke when it arrived and the smoke and noise when it left! Remarkably two weeks later their second CV-880, N48059, appeared on August 4ᵗʰ (KM780 from Malta). Sadly these were the only visits of the Convair CV-880 to Manchester and although they'd been around since 1959, they weren't considered a success. The only major airlines operating them were Cathay Pacific, JAL, Delta & TWA, none of which made it into Manchester. *(Geoff Ball)*

November 11ᵗʰ 1978. One of the highlights from the previous day's batch of extensive diversions was US Navy C-9A 160049 'City of Jacksonville'. It was an Upper Heyford diversion, carrying a number of Admirals. It nearly didn't make it into Manchester as the Airport had decided not to accept anymore diversions, except for Concorde if requested, which was later rescinded. This shot shows it parked on the Domestic pier, with its thrust reversers still open. *(Ian Barrie)*

July 1ˢᵗ 1978. After several years of planning and false starts, Manchester's own based cargo airline, Pelican Air Transport, began operations. Boeing 707 G-BPAT departed at 1555 today as DP2001 bound for N'dola, Zambia via Athens, before returning on the 10ᵗʰ with 33 tonnes of grapes from Cyprus. Employing fifty-two staff, the airline added a second Boeing 707, G-BEVN in October. However, the airline soon found it could operate more regular and lucrative work elsewhere, mainly out of Gatwick and Ostend. From the end of 1978, visits to Manchester by the airline were at a premium, and by 1982 the airline had ceased trading. *(MIA Archive Collection)*

September 5ᵗʰ 1979. This extremely smart Douglas DC-3, HZ-TA3, arrived on a sunny Wednesday afternoon en route from Houston to Riyadh, due to a shortage of the appropriate fuel at Prestwick. The aircraft which has been purchased by a Saudi Sheik and has a full VIP interior is seen here on delivery to Saudi Arabia. *(Geoff Ball)*

September 12th 1979. This day saw the inaugural flight of Northwest Orient's twice-weekly Amsterdam-Manchester-New York freight service, with Boeing 747-251F N616US operating the first flight as 'Northwest 923'. The airline operated the service until September 1981, when they decided to transfer the flights to Gatwick. This meant they could concentrate their UK operations at Gatwick and Prestwick, where they also had passenger services. *(Geoff Ball)*

October 28th 1979. British Airways began their Shuttle Service between Manchester-London, complementing their existing services between London-Glasgow/Edinburgh & Belfast. An hourly service operated at peak times and a two-hourly service at other times. The check-in time was reduced to ten minutes before departure and it was guaranteed that if the main flight was full a back-up plane would be made available - even for just one passenger! Dragon Rapide G-AKOE was brought in to help promote the new service. *(MIA Archive Collection)*

November 21ˢᵗ 1979. Heathrow and Gatwick had been badly affected by fog over the last forty-eight hours and for much of that time so had Manchester, but by the afternoon it had cleared sufficiently to start accepting diversions. One such aircraft was colourful Braniff International B.747-227B N602BN, seen here having recently arrived as BN602 from Dallas-Fort Worth. This was the penultimate visit by the airline, as they had ceased trading by May 1982. *(Mark White)*

November 27ᵗʰ 1979. An everyday scene at the Airport's Control Tower, operating since its construction in 1962, as part of the new Terminal. A brand new tower on the south-west side of the airfield was completed in 2013. *(MIA Archive Collection)*

1980. Northern Executive began operations in May 1962 with a single PA-28 Cherokee, G-ARVS. On display are four of their air taxi fleet, including their latest addition, personalized Lear Jet 35 G-LEAR. The Lear Jet was used for general charters and as an air ambulance. *(MIA Archive Collection)*

February 21st 1980. Martinair DC-10 PH-MBG arrived with an inbound load of 50 tonnes of tomatoes. It would normally be operated through Stansted, but it was required for an unusual outbound cargo. The Foreign Office had commandeered ten Bell Jet Ranger helicopters, ultimately bound for Rhodesia, to assist in the supervision of elections. The charter company chose Manchester because of its central location, due to the helicopters arriving from all over the UK. *(Geoff Ball)*

April 27ᵗʰ 1980. Up to this point all visits by Concorde had been British Airways diversions, but on this warm Sunday morning Manchester Airport was swamped by 40,000 visitors ready to witness the 0956 arrival of the first commercial Concorde flight. The event caused overflowing car parks and gridlocked roads when hundreds parked illegally around the airport. F-BVFB had been chartered French car company Renault, as a special thank you to its 200 UK dealers. *(MIA Archive Collection)*

June 1ˢᵗ 1980. This was the occasion of the first Soviet-bloc airline to start a scheduled service from Manchester. Polish-airline LOT began a twice-weekly service to Warsaw with TU-134s, with SP-LHD operating the inaugural flight. These flights ended in October 1981 due to increasing political tensions within the country. Also in 1980, Aeroflot operated a fortnightly charter flight to Leningrad on behalf of holiday-firm Intourist. *(MIA Archive Collection)*

August 31st 1981. Bank Holidays rarely produced interesting visitors, but the first ever visit of a USAF C-141B Starlifter, 40629, bucked that trend! It arrived direct from Charleston AFB, South Carolina, with ninety troops in full combat gear, who were transported onwards to RAF Burtonwood on two corporation buses. As the aircraft was also carrying a hazardous cargo, it was parked on Taxiway 3, close to the Fire Station. *(MIA Archive Collection)*

October 16th 1981. The visit of USAF VC-135B 62-4127, which arrived from RAF Wittering, was the second of its type this month. Converted as a VIP aircraft, it served with the 89th Military Air Wing based at Andrews AFB, Maryland. *(Geoff Ball)*

December 11ᵗʰ 1981. This day was notable for its extreme wintery weather, lots of sunshine, snow and very cold temperatures, but fog was the reason for the three British Caledonian DC-10s diverting into Manchester, adding to the previous day's arrivals. Heavy overnight snow and very low temperatures locked them onto their stands for much longer than anticipated! *(Paul Rowland)*

January 24ᵗʰ 1982. The first visit of the shortened version of the popular Boeing 747, the B.747SP (Special Performance), was also the result of fog at Heathrow. Arriving at 0920 (SA236 from Sal Island), it was in a revised colour scheme of English writing on the port side and Afrikaans on the starboard side. Unfortunately the aircraft proved to be unsuccessful. Just forty-five were built and only eight different aircraft ever visited Manchester. *(Andy Hall)*

May 27th 1982. British Caledonian Helicopters Sikorsky S-61 G-BHPU & G-BFPF called in for fuel en route Aberdeen-Gatwick. They were the papal transport for Pope John Paul II's visit to the UK from May 28th to June 2nd. *(Geoff Ball)*

1982. A busy summer Sunday on Manchester Airport's excellent terraces. *(MIA Archive Collection)*

July 17th 1982. Another attempt to base an airline at Manchester was made by Sureway Travel, forming Air Manchester to rescue thousands of holidays since Laker's collapse. They bought BAC 1-11 G-SURE at a knockdown price of £1.2million and began operations in June 1982. *(Geoff Ball)*

August 1982. Happy holidaymakers are pictured aboard Air Manchester BAC 1-11 G-SURE, but by September the airline were having licensing problems with the Spanish authorities and by October the warning bells were ringing. They made drastic staff cuts and moved operations to Liverpool after negotiating cheaper landing charges. All flights were ceased during November and they were put up for sale by their parent company, Pennine Commercial Holdings. *(MIA Archive Collection)*

June 7th 1983. Seen on the climb-out, having just performed an ILS and overshoot at 1046 on a very grey morning was NASA B.747 N905NA, with Space Shuttle Enterprise on its back. They were en route back to the USA, via Keflavik after appearing at the Paris Air Show. They also performed overshoots at Birmingham and Glasgow on their way home. *(Geoff Ball)*

September 10th 1984. Boeing sent in their company Boeing 737-300 demonstrator, N352AU, on behalf of Orion Airways for publicity purposes following their order for four aircraft. Airport chiefs were positively glowing about the aircraft, which was so quiet on departure it didn't even register on the noise monitor! This B.737 variant became extremely popular with airlines and travellers alike. *(MIA Archive Collection)*

September 30th 1984. Qantas Boeing 747-238 VH-EBG. One of several breakthroughs in bilateral agreements achieved by Airport Director Gil Thompson was the commencement of direct services to Australia. Qantas began flights on April 1st 1983, initially twice-weekly serving Sydney and Melbourne. By October 1992 they were operating daily flights via Heathrow. *(Geoff Ball)*

May 22nd 1985. The Bristol 170 Freighter had completely disappeared from Europe during the early 1970s, but still proved its worth in rugged areas such as Canada and Australia. This venerable machine, G-BISU, was delivered to Instone Airlines in 1981 after an 87-hour ferry flight from Australia. G-BISU which is seen operating an outbound freight flight to Antwerp, served with the airline until 1987, when it was donated to Imperial War Museum at Duxford. *(Geoff Ball)*

December 31ˢᵗ 1985. This was the final Trident flight through Manchester, operated by G-AWZO. Arriving on a Shuttle flight, it departed later with 146 passengers on a much publicised 'farewell flight', carrying out overshoots at Liverpool, Ronaldsway and Manchester before returning an hour later. Each lucky passenger was presented with a box of chocolates, a certificate and a card listing the major landmarks in the aircraft's history. It departed back to Heathrow at 1832 operating BA4513 and was jointly the last scheduled Trident service, an honour shared with G-AWZU (BA635 Copenhagen-LHR). Both aircraft landed at Heathrow at the same time on parallel runways, officially timed at 1908. *(Above Mark Duffy, below Geoff Ball)*

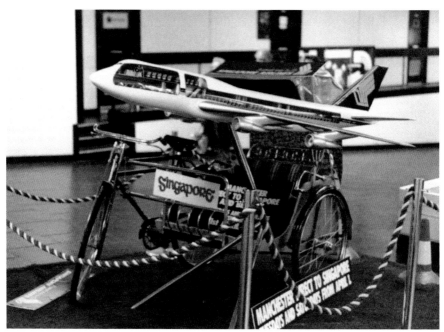

April 1ˢᵗ 1986. Part of the publicity display inside the main terminal promoting today's inaugural flight by Singapore Airlines. Another long and bitter fight was won to finally attract the airline to operate a twice-weekly service, with the first service being operated by B.747-312 Combi 9V-SKM. The airline still serves Manchester today, operating a daily Boeing 777-300 service via Munich. *(MIA Archive Collection)*

1986. The entire Cal-Air fleet could be seen on Friday afternoons during the summer. One was based, one operated a 'w' pattern from/to Ibiza and the third was a Gatwick-Manchester-Orlando charter. In 1988, the airline was branded as Novair, but ceased trading in 1990. *(Peter Hampson)*

May 4th 1986. Manchester played host to many participants at the nearby Barton Air Show, but arguably none as rare as this pair of Lockheed F-104 Starfighters, operated by the German Air Force. They arrived after performing a stunning display of speed and agility and are seen here night-stopping on the Dan-Air apron. Their departure off Runway 24 was equally spectacular. They came back round to perform a fast run down Runway 06, before eventually going vertically upwards to 15,000ft, which was achieved before they had even reached nearby Heald Green! *(Geoff Ball)*

May 6th 1987. Iraqi Airways Ilyushin IL-76 YI-ANC was a first visit of type, but it arrived a week later than anticipated and stayed for two days. In view of the Iraq-Iran conflict going on at the time the crew were very cagey about what they were up to, apparently uploading a consignment of lubrication oil. After all the attention it received, it was thought they wouldn't visit again, but this proved to be incorrect as there were six such flights between May 1987-March 1989 *(Geoff Ball)*

1987. Air 2000 Boeing 757-28A G-OOOA seen departing on another holiday flight in their original livery. This was the first of fourteen aircraft operated by the Manchester-based airline until their takeover in 2004. *(MIA Archive Collection)*

1987. Direct freight services to the USA had been tried before, both with Northwest Orient and then Air Express International. Emery Worldwide began daily flights to New York on May 15th 1985 and such was their success, two flights a day were operated on occasion, as seen in this photograph. This frequency was maintained until 1992, when it was reduced to twice-weekly, before disappearing altogether by 1993. *(Peter Hampson)*

February 18th 1987. Probably more recognisable in military markings, the Boeing CH-47 Chinook made its first visit to Manchester on this day. G-BISN operated by British International Helicopters, was the only civilian example to land at Manchester, arriving from its Aberdeen base operating oil rig-related flights. Although it was using Manchester as a base for a mission in the Pennines, the aircraft spent most of the two days inside the old British Airways hangar. *(MIA Archive Collection)*

April 3rd 1988. Federal Express DC-10F N312FE arrived from Newark for a handling trial. Manchester was being assessed as a diversionary airfield for the parcels giant, who were commencing flights to Brussels. *(Geoff Ball)*

June 24th 1988. Manchester Airport took a nostalgic step back into the 1930s today, with the arrival of Douglas DC-3 PH-DDA at 1515, exactly fifty years since the first airliner landed, which happened to be KLM Douglas DC-2 PH-AKP which had also touched down the day before for the airport's festivities on Saturday 25th June 1988. To celebrate the occasion, dignitaries from the City of Manchester and airport VIPs were onboard. After landing KLM presented the airport with a commemorative gift. *(MIA Archive Collection)*

June 25th 1988. It seemed that no aviation commemoration could be complete without the last remaining Avro Lancaster. PA474 was in attendance with the other two aircraft that formed the Battle of Britain Memorial Flight, Hurricane LF363 & Spitfire Mk.IIA P7350. *(MIA Archive Collection)*

June 25th 1988. Manchester-Ringway had been operating a year earlier than the official date. Fairey Aviation had an opening day on June 8th 1937, on completion of their hangar for the final assembly of Fairey Battles. Flying demonstrations took place on a completed part of the landing area on the western side, but the first recorded flight was DH.Hornet Moth G-ADND, piloted by Fairey test pilot Duncan Menzies on May 17th 1937. It arrived for the celebrations in immaculate condition and made an excellent subject for photographers. *(MIA Archive Collection)*

May 28th 1989. RAF Vulcan XH558 which has just arrived to night-stop after performing at the Barton Air Show is seen delicately navigating the taxiways. It was also the first Vulcan to land at Manchester since XM610 diverted in from Woodford on January 24th 1964! *(Peter Hampson)*

October 3rd 1989. Catalina JV928 G-BLSC arrived for Dan-Air Engineering, to have authentic gun blisters installed, before finally departing on January 9th 1990. Made in 1945, it was one of 2,000 built for the US Navy with the RAF operating a further 578, but despite its serial it never operated for the RAF. Tragically this aircraft crashed and ultimately sank at Southampton Water in July 1998. *(Peter Hampson)*

October 20th 1989. Air Hong Kong began their twice-weekly cargo operations with Boeing 707F VR-HKL. The flight initially operated Hong Kong-Bahrain-Manchester-Paris-Bahrain-Bangkok-Hong Kong and had a capacity of up to 40 tonnes of cargo. Boeing 747-200s took over the operation in July 1981 and increased the frequency to five-weekly. *(Geoff Ball)*

November 14th 1989. A selection of diverted aircraft from the previous day, demonstrating exactly what an international pier should look like! From back to front: Virgin Atlantic B.747 G-VIRG (VIR078 from Orlando), Ethiopian B.767 ET-AIZ (ETH710 from Addis Ababa/Rome), Britannia Airways B.767 G-BOPB, Nigeria Airways DC-10 5N-ANN (NGA802 from Kano), BWIA Tristar 500 9Y-TGJ (BWA900 from Bridgetown) and Cyprus Airways A.310 5B-DAS (CYP504 from Paphos). *(Geoff Ball)*

January 1990. Work began on Qualitair's large maintenance hangar in July 1988, with the first of four roof sections hoisted into place on January 30th 1989. In August 1989, the company was bought out by Swedish company FFV Aerotech, later becoming FLS. The new hangar was opened on October 18th and this 1990 photograph shows the sheer size and gives an idea of the number of aircraft it can handle at any one time. *(Peter Hampson)*

August 27th 1990. One of the most colourful and striking South Side residents around at this time was worn by this 1972-built Cessna FRA.150L Aerobat, G-AZJY. *(Geoff Ball)*

December 1990. Jetstar S9-NAE is sat inside the FLS hangar in immaculate condition. Arriving on November 18th 1990 for storage, it departed as VR-CCY on March 13th 1992. *(Barry Swann)*

1991. Work on the airports brand new railway station is at a well-advanced stage, linked by a spur off the Manchester-Wilmslow via Heald Green main line. It opened in May 1993 with three platforms, directly linking passengers to Cumbria, Yorkshire & North-East. *(MIA Archive Collection)*

April 1991. Four of the five brand new McDonnell Douglas MD-83s delivered over the last few months to new UK holiday company Airtours. The Rossendale-based tour company timed their existence to perfection, plugging the gap in the holiday market following the demise of Air Europe two months earlier. *(Peter Hampson)*

61

May 17ᵗʰ 1991. A superb airborne shot of RAE Canberra B.6 WK163 arriving from Brize Norton for display at the Barton Air Show two days later. On August 28ᵗʰ 1957 this 1954 Woodford-built aircraft set a world altitude record of 70,300ft. *(Geoff Ball)*

May 20ᵗʰ 1991. RAF Shackleton AEW.2 WL790 arrived from RAF Lossiemouth with spares for fellow Shackleton, 'broken' WR960. The latter aircraft had arrived the previous afternoon to perform at the Barton Air Show, but after going tech on arrival it was unable to perform. *(Peter Hampson)*

May 1991. Looking magnificent inside the FLS hangar is Bogazici Boeing 707-321 TC-JCF. It had arrived the previous month for storage, having been used as a cargo aircraft for THY. It stuck around until June 28th, when it departed for Miami in all-white colours. *(Barry Swann)*

June 29th 1991. After five years of hard work, Delta finally commenced a daily service to Atlanta on June 27th 1991. Here two days later, Boeing 767-300 N176DN is seen operating the flight DAL064/5. In June 1997, they also added a daily flight to New York. *(Geoff Ball)*

July 12th 1991. One of the highlights of the year was today's appearance of Chosonminhang Ilyushin IL-62 P-885, arriving with the team for the World Student Games taking place in Sheffield. A request for a landing slot was made the previous morning, but after neglecting to obtain the necessary diplomatic clearance their arrival was delayed by 24 hours. They made the return visit on July 26th to pick up the team. *(Above Geoff Ball)*. "See you again in two weeks!" *(Below Ian Barrie)*

September 30th 1991. UR 82008 is seen making its first visit to Manchester. The giant Russian transport plane, Antonov AN-124 arrived from Dubai with a 36-tonne piece of gearbox from the Supertanker MV Nobo Frontier, which had broken down in Dubai. Once the cargo was carefully unloaded, it was craned onto the back of a lorry and transported to David Browns in Huddersfield for repair. *(Geoff Ball)*

February 8th 1992. In an incredible month for weather diversions, this day saw the record for the highest number of wide-bodies on the ground at Manchester at the same time broken. Thirty were on the ground at once, including twenty Boeing 747s which was also a record. The seven tails pictured above had arrived from all corners of the globe. *(Paul Rowland)*

1992. This panoramic aerial view shows the first phase construction of Terminal 2 taking shape and the ground cleared for the full extent of the project to be realised. Singapore and South African B.747s can be seen in the background on Pier C and various aircraft congregated on the remote stands around the FLS hangar include a PIA B.747 which had gone tech the previous evening. *(MIA Archive Collection)*

April 5th 1992. American Airlines began a daily Chicago flight with Boeing 767s on May 1st 1986. Since then they've served Boston, Dallas, Miami & New York and operated a second daily flight to Chicago. On this date they introduced the MD-11 onto the route, with N1753, seen here taxiing out as AAL055 on the first flight. *(MIA Archive Collection)*

May 24th 1992. Immaculate looking Meteor NF-11 G-LOSM/WM167 arrived two days earlier with several other aircraft to take part in the press call, prior to the weekend's Barton Air Show. *(Geoff Ball)*

June 19ᵗʰ 1992. This photograph with BAC 1-11 G-AVMT in the forefront, has two contrasting factors attached it. Firstly, Terminal 2 looks complete, although it had some way to go as interior work was still ongoing. Secondly, it marked the final year of the Airport's affiliation with the British Airways fleet of Super 1-11s. Their links to Manchester began in 1969 when they started appearing on the airline's schedules and from 1971 to 1977 when they were officially based, they became 'Manchester's airline'. G-AVMW operated the last flight from Manchester when it flew a Santa Special on December 24ᵗʰ 1992. *(Rick Ward)*

August 19ᵗʰ 1992. This line-up shows three Aeroflot Ilyushin Il-76s, CCCP-76785, 76470 & 76812. The first two which were operating a charter for British Nuclear Fuels, carrying low grade nuclear waste, had been delayed for a week due to objections. The third was part of a Simon-Carves contract taking out equipment to a plastics factory in Ervan, Armenia. *(Michael Wait)*

1993. The go-ahead for Terminal 2 was given in January 1990, with work commencing the following month. It was finally completed in early 1993 and officially opened by the Duke of Edinburgh on May 5th 1993. *(MIA Archive Collection)*

March 23rd 1993. This was the scene just two days prior to the official opening of T2 by the Duke of Edinburgh, twenty-one years after he opened the present 1962 terminal. It shows two airlines that have passed into history. In 2000 the Thomson group was acquired by TUI of Germany and by 2004 had re-branded Britannia Airways as Thomson and Air 2000 were re-named First Choice Airways also in 2004. *(Geoff Ball)*

May 2nd 1993. A very rare type to visit Manchester, mainly because only ten production aircraft were ever built, was the VFW-Fokker 614. German Air Force example 17+02 had arrived from Cologne to pick a group of soldiers. The only other to visit was Air Alsace F-GATG back on February 1st 1978. *(Geoff Ball)*

June 18th 1993. MD90 Demonstrator N901DC arrived from Stockholm as part of its European tour, which included the Paris Air Show. Its only appearance in the UK was at Manchester, to be demonstrated to Airtours. It operated two local flights, mainly with Airtours employees onboard. It departed back Stateside the following day, but the only European operator to order the type was Scandinavian Airlines. *(MIA Archive Collection)*

July 11th 1993. Gulf Air Boeing 767-3P6 A40-GU. Gulf Air could be classed as the forerunner to the explosion of flights to the Middle East that we have today, although the airline itself had a modest operation. They began a twice-weekly service to Abu Dhabi via Frankfurt on October 25th 1992, which lasted until March 1996. *(Geoff Ball)*

July 17th 1993. Okada Air had been a familiar sight at Manchester, sending in their second-hand BAC 1-11s through Dan-Air for maintenance. They also sent in their SE.210 Caravelle in February 1985. Former Japan Airlines Boeing 747-146 5N-EDO first appeared in June 1992 and again in March 1993 for attention with FLS for attention. This time it was placed into storage at various parts of the airfields, until finally departing on February 20th 1994. *(Geoff Ball)*

1993. An aerial view of Manchester Airport and the surrounding areas, a sight which was to change forever. After an exhaustive public enquiry which took place between June 1994 and 1995, the go-ahead was given on January 15th to the planning approval of the £200million Runway 2. After various objections site clearance began in September 1997, which amongst other things meant the demolition of the South Side hangars. Work was completed by 2000 and the runway (06R/24L – as it was known at the time) was open for business in February 2001. The first aircraft to use the new Runway 24L on a commercial flight was Emirates A.330 A6-EAB, departing at 1411 on February 5th 2001. *(MIA Archive Collection)*

January 4th 1994. Airbus A.340-311 G-VAEL is making a first visit of type, positioning in from Gatwick to operate a sub-charter to Orlando for Leisure International *(Stuart Prince)*

September 16th 1994. This JU-52, one of the first all-metal designs manufactured by Junkers, has had a mixed history of fortunes. During the war it was seized by the Luftwaffe and converted to military use, but by 1945 it was badly corroded and some of its parts were used to create a new JU.52 aircraft. After flying in Norway until 1956, it was sold to an airline in Ecuador, but by 1962 after being abandoned at Quito it became a nesting site for birds, but was eventually restored by Lufthansa. *(Lee Collins)*

November 1st 1994. This was the only visit to Manchester of an Antonov AN-28. SP-PDF was actually a Polish-built example and was returning home from a sales tour of South America, particularly Colombia, where it attracted a little more attention than usual from Customs & Excise! The type first flew in 1969 and a total of 191 were built. *(Lee Collins)*

December 2nd 1994. This was the inaugural flight of Aer Lingus' five-times-weekly flight from/to New York via Shannon. Operated by Airbus A.330s, the airline stepped into the gap left by American Airlines who ceased their New York operation for the winter. The service however only lasted until April the following year. *(MIA Archive Collection)*

August 26th 1995. Qatar Airways Boeing 747SR-81 A7-ABK was one of two operated by the airline. It arrived at Manchester from Marana via Tucson for fitment of a new interior with FLS. It had previously been operated by All Nippon in a high-density layout and would eventually inaugurate services from London-Gatwick later that year. *(Geoff Ball)*

September 16th 1995. Lockheed C141B Starlifter 65-0222 arrived at Manchester as 'Elvis 14', bringing British servicemen back from the States after finishing exercises. As it was getting ready to leave on the Sunday with all engines running, the slot was put back a few minutes, so the Loadmaster proceeded to take time out on the tarmac by jokingly lying down in front of the aircraft. It departed ten minutes later with the same call-sign Elvis 14. It was a truly wonderful aircraft, with very friendly crew. *(Michael Oldham)*

October 18th 1995. The only visit to Manchester so far by Philippine Airlines took place when Douglas DC-10 RP-C2114 arrived for attention with FLS. It's seen here being prepared for a test flight prior to its departure to Frankfurt. *(Geoff Ball)*

December 2nd 1995. The Royal Air Force operated seven Boeing E-3As as Airborne Early Warning Control (AWACS), which were effectively up-rated B.707s. They had been regular visitors to Manchester since 1993, operating training flights but never landing, so the arrival of ZH104 the previous evening effectively made it a first visit of type. It made an abortive attempt to return to Waddington on this day, but eventually left two days later on an operational mission bound for Aviano AFB. *(MIA Archive Collection)*

December 11th 1995. The undoubted pick of today's forty-five weather diversions was the arrival of Boeing 747-2J6B B-2448 (CCA937 from Peking). This was not only the airline's first visit to Manchester, but also the first Chinese-registered aircraft to visit Manchester. *(Paul Rowland)*

March 22nd 1996. A name from the past returned to Manchester fourteen years later! Laker, which was still operated by Sir Freddie Laker, had been operating in the USA for a while with B.727s from Florida to the Bahamas. He needed FAA clearance to operate transatlantic flights again, which included some proving flights. The first proving flight operated on this date with DC-10 N832LA and the first scheduled flight to Orlando operated on April 9th with DC-10 N833LA. *(Geoff Ball)*

May 17th 1996. With all the razzamatazz and publicity that we have come to expect from Richard Branson, he was at Manchester on the day of the inaugural flight of Virgin Atlantic's new six-times-weekly flight to Orlando, with the first flight being operated by Airbus A.340-311 G-VSUN. The flights now operate daily with Airbus A330s, supplemented in the summer months with an extra B.747-400 flight on certain days. *(MIA Archive Collection)*

June 12th 1996. Amongst the Euro '96 traffic this month was this outstanding visitor, Japanese Air Force Boeing 747-47C 20-1101. It was 'checking out' the facilities at Manchester ahead of a G7 summit due to take place in Birmingham later in the year, just in case there was a problem at Birmingham. The Japanese are very superstitious and won't send Royals or dignitaries into an airfield unless one of their aircraft has already been there! *(Lee Collins)*

June 20th 1996. Ilyushin IL-86 RA-86123, which arrived to take Russian fans home after being eliminated from Euro '96, was making its second visit after bringing fans in eight days earlier. Other IL-86 visits in connection with the tournament during the month were RA-86054 (12th) & RA86096 (20th). To date, these have been the only Ilyushin IL-86s to visit Manchester. *(Geoff Ball)*

July 4th 1996. The second B.777-21H for Emirates, A6-EME, was delivered via Manchester today. Whilst en route from the Boeing factory in Seattle, it was forced to divert to Keflavik with a port Trent engine problem, before eventually arriving at Manchester six hours late. It was due to carry on to Dubai with various VIPs, but the problem was serious enough for it to be towed to the British Airways hangar awaiting a part due to be flown up from East Midlands. It finally departed the following day but had to collect passengers from Heathrow on the way after their other B.777, A6-EMD, also developed tech problems and became stuck at Larnaca! *(Lee Collins)*

August 17th 1996. Delta had steadily built up their daily Atlanta service since its introduction in June 1991 and less than twelve months later they were operating Lockheed Tristars on the route. In June 1997 they also began operating a daily New York service and in June 1998 they upgraded the Atlanta route again, this time to the larger MD-11. This particular MD-11, N812DE, which is in special Olympic colours, had arrived earlier that morning due to fog at Gatwick. *(Stuart Prince)*

January 15th 1997. Brazilian airline Varig made their first visit today when MD-11 PP-VOQ arrived from Sao Paolo as RG756 due to fog, as did thirty-five other diversions from various parts of the UK. This was also the day the government finally approved the building of Runway 2. *(Michael Oldham)*

April 1997. Airport and airline staff are celebrating Singapore Airlines' expansion of services, after building the route up since starting their twice-weekly service in 1986. *(MIA Archive Collection)*

May 27th 1997. Several 'exotic' Dash-8s were delivered through Manchester during the late-1990s. The second of two appearing during the month was of Air Niugini P2-ANK, making a forty-seven minute visit whilst routing Reykjavik-Bastia. *(Geoff Ball)*

April 15th 1998. Cubana Ilyushin IL-62M CU-T1280. One of the more interesting routes commencing during the decade was the introduction of a weekly flight to Havana by national airline Cubana. The service which began on December 19th 1997 was operated by AOM Douglas DC-10s initially. Between March and October Ilyushin IL-62s were regularly used, but reverted to DC-10s again after the service was terminated in January 1999. *(Nik French)*

July 13th 1998. Nine different airlines can be seen lined up on this busy Monday morning. They include two Chicago flights by American Airlines, two Delta flights to Atlanta and New York respectively and two Pegasus charter flights, both to Dalaman. *(Geoff Ball)*

October 3rd 1998. Finnair MD-11 OH-LGA positioned from Helsinki to operate flight SCY761/2, a sub-charter on behalf of Air Scandic to/from Alicante. Normally employed to operate the airline's long-haul routes, this was the only Finnair MD-11 to visit Manchester. *(Geoff Ball)*

November 4th 1998. A double first visit of type took place when Maersk B.737-700s OY-MRB & OY-MRC arrived from Copenhagen bringing in Brondby fans for their European Cup match with Manchester United. The airline also operated a scheduled service to Copenhagen between November 2004 and October 2005. *(Geoff Ball)*

November 7th 1998. Trans Arabian Air Transport began the first of a series of regular flights on July 16th 1998, bringing in fresh fish from Mwanza, Tanzania via Khartoum. However, the schedule of these flights became erratic due to the phases of the moon encouraging the fish to bite! Occasionally two flights in a day would operate, as can be seen in this shot, with the last operating in March 1999. *(Lee Collins)*

February 20th 1999. Boeing 727-230 HC-BZS routed via Manchester on delivery to TAME of Ecuador. It ended up going tech on arrival and night-stopped, before its onward flight, initially bound for Keflavik. Formerly operated by Istanbul Airlines, this was the first Ecuadorean registered aircraft to visit Manchester. *(Nik French)*

April 28th 1999. The Virgin Group branched out into the holiday charter market in 1999 with two Airbus A.320s. G-VMED made the airline's first visit on this date, making a series of local flights before their summer programme started on May 1st with a flight to Alicante. However, this was another short-lived venture and ceased trading in October 2001. *(Rick Ward)*

May 16th 1999. The Grumman Goose hadn't been seen since the 1960s, when the Airport could boast two based examples. G-ASCS was operated by Ferranti and G-ASXG by the Duke of Westminster. This example, N4575C, was routing Woodford-Luton. It's still flying in 2013 and is currently based at Weston, Ireland. *(Geoff Ball)*

May 26th 1999. French airline Corsair was often seen at Manchester during the 1990s, mainly transporting football fans to or from Manchester to follow the Red Devils. They operated a single B.747SP which was rarely used, but on this occasion F-GTOM was one of many Corsair aircraft bringing jubilant United fans back from Barcelona after winning the European Cup. *(Lee Collins)*

May 27th 1999. Having won the European Cup for the first time in thirty one years, the Airport was involved with the return of masses of Manchester United fans from Barcelona. This was the scene during the morning with five Corsair aircraft in view, each making two or three round trips on a day when the Airport handled the most movements in a single day, totalling 701. *(Nik French)*

July 4th 1999. Czech Air Force Tupolev TU-154 0601 operated from/to Prague, transporting a party of war veterans into Manchester. *(Geoff Ball)*

November 21ˢᵗ 1999. Continental Airlines introduced a daily Boeing 757 Newark service on July 20ᵗʰ 1995, and similarly built the route up over the next few years. By September 1999, it was operated by Douglas DC-10s, but these were being phased out during the month as Boeing 777s began operating. B.777-212 N77014 is seen here taxiing out for departure as COA021 in special 'Peter Max' colours. *(Geoff Ball)*

2000. Cathay Pacific Boeing 747-467 VR-HOX is pictured wearing 'Same Team, Same Dream - Spirit of Hong Kong' colours. The airline began a twice-weekly service to Hong Kong on October 31ˢᵗ 1989 with Boeing 747-467 VR-HOO. This might have been the first visit by the B.747-400 but they were pipped by Qantas, who sent in VH-OJC a day earlier! In November 1993, this became a daily B.747-400 service, but it ended on July 9ᵗʰ 2001. *(Nik French)*

February 10th 2000. This night shot shows the first visit of the extended Boeing 757, the B.757-300. N1002R was the Boeing demonstrator, but destined to become D-ABOI with Condor. It did a demonstration flight to Air 2000, Airtours and JMC before leaving for Luton. *(Geoff Ball)*

May 27th 2000. Citybird 'The Flying Dream' was a Belgium airline that operated out of Brussels between 1996 and 2001, with Boeing 737-400s, MD-11s, A.300s and B.767s. Seen here is Boeing 767 OO-CTG arriving on a trooping charter from RAF Akrotiri. *(Geoff Ball)*

March 10ᵗʰ 2001. Casa CN-235 No.253 is one of two aircraft operated by the Irish Air Corps, but not often seen at Manchester. This aircraft was routing Newcastle-Luton on a training flight. *(Geoff Ball)*

May 28ᵗʰ 2003. Thank goodness for wide-angled lenses! Seen here is just a selection of the aircraft used in the mass invasion of Italian supporters, which had arrived for the Champions League Final at Old Trafford between AC Milan and Juventus. *(Terry Shone)*

May 28th 2003. The Champions League Final also created huge crowds to Manchester Airport. The first arrival connected with the match was Volare Airbus A.330 I-VLEH on May 26th carrying the AC Milan team. This was closely followed by Blue Panorama B.737 EI-CUN with the Juventus team. Between the 26th and the 29th there were 469 extra movements and the 28th recorded 889 movements in a single day, which was another record. (*Above Paul Rowland, below Rick Ward*)

November 2003. In April 2003 Air France and British Airways announced that they would retire their Concorde fleet by the end of the year. They said that passengers had never recovered since the Air France Concorde crash of July 2000. In October 2003, there were a series of farewell flights from Heathrow, including one to Manchester on the 22nd with G-BOAG. The final retirement of all Concorde aircraft followed two days later. Meanwhile, there were rumours that a Concorde was to be preserved at Manchester, which became fact when G-BOAC arrived at 1053 on October 31st 2003. Over fifty press staff attended and a large numbers of spectators. Later on it was towed near to the Viewing Park where decommissioning began. Once the security fence had been temporarily taken down, Concorde was on the move ready for positioning. The picture below shows Concorde in position during the pre-hangar days *(Both photos Alan Jones)*

August 27ᵗʰ 2004. The fantastic sight and sound of the first Antonov AN-22 to visit was UR-09307 due to a First Choice Airbus A.321 going tech in Lanzarote. The Antonov was used to fly out a replacement engine, before returning to Manchester two days later with the duff engine. So far this is the only one to visit. *(Stuart Prince)*

January 22ⁿᵈ 2005. Boeing 707-330B N88ZL. A cold and frosty Saturday morning witnessed the very last visit to Manchester of a civilian Boeing 707. Formerly ex-Lufthansa D-ABUB, it was now operating for LOWA as a VIP charter aircraft. It arrived at 0625 from Riyadh and is seen departing four hours later bound for Miami. *(Denis Norman)*

May 25th 2005. Airbus A.330 G-MDBD is seen completing its pushback on a wet, miserable morning. By 2005, the MyTravel group were carrying 3.5 million holidaymakers a year from the UK, but in February 2007 amid worsening financial conditions, they agreed a merger with Thomas Cook, which meant that the MyTravel colours would disappear, after choosing to adopt the Thomas Cook brand on its fleet of aircraft. *(Geoff Ball)*

October 30th 2005. Visits by DC-8s dwindled during the decade but African International Douglas DC-8-62F ZS-OZV was a most welcome sight. It's seen operating the second of three cargo flights to Islamabad on behalf of PIA during late October/early November 2005. *(Geoff Ball)*

May 6th 2006. Sky Europe Boeing 737-53C OM-SEE. The airline began operations from Manchester on April 9th 2005, with a three-times-weekly service to Bratislava. In April 2006 they started introducing brand new B.737-700s to the route, but financial troubles in January 2009 saw the airline having to return six of these aircraft. The continuing cost of leasing aircraft to cover its routes across Europe made their position untenable and they ceased operations in September 2009. *(Geoff Ball)*

May 6th 2006. The shape of things to come! Lufthansa Cargo MD-11 D-ALCC was operating a one-off freight charter from/to Frankfurt, but in November 2009 they started a twice-weekly New York-Manchester-Frankfurt freight service. In 2013, these flights continue but are now operating three-times-weekly. *(Geoff Ball)*

July 19th 2006. Syrian Arab commenced services to Damascus from Manchester in June 2004, scheduled to be operated by Airbus A.320s. However, the airlines two Boeing 747SPs YK-AHA & YK-AHB were frequent visitors in the four years they operated the route. This was also the only occasion the type was use on scheduled flights out of Manchester. *(Nik French)*

September 16th 2006. I trust you've paid your entrance fees to the Aviation Viewing Park? *(Geoff Ball)*

October 1st 2006. The month got off to an excellent start with the arrival of Antonov AN-225 UR-82060, the largest aircraft in the world! Originally designed to carry the Russian Space Shuttle back in the 1980s, this prototype after being grounded for many years was modified for heavy cargo operations and placed back into service in 2001. It was in great demand, transporting objects once thought impossible to move by air, such as locomotives and 150-ton generators. It also proved to be a valuable asset to international relief organisations for its ability to quickly transport huge quantities of emergency supplies. Its visit to Manchester was to airlift stage equipment for a Snoop Dog concert in Lagos, Nigeria and was scheduled to depart two days later. However, there were numerous delays with the loading of the trucks and equipment and it didn't leave until the 5th. *(Nik French)*

April 24th 2007. Air Berlin began operation from Manchester on November 1st 2004, not with one flight, but four! Destinations served from this date were Berlin, Dusseldorf, Hamburg & Paderborn. Between then and the time of this photo, the schedules were constantly changing and the Boeing 737-800s were being supplemented by new Airbus A.319s. *(Michael Oldham)*

May 3rd 2007. After over forty years of regularity at Manchester Airport, this was the final visit of a BAC 1-11. Privately-owned YR-MIA arrived from Paris-Le Bourget two days earlier and is seen sat in the morning sunshine, before later departing for Newcastle. *(Nik French)*

June 1st 2007. Boeing 747-412F B-2428. Great Wall Cargo operated up to four weekly flights between Manchester and Shanghai via Amsterdam from May 2007 and March 2009. In 2011, they were merged into China Cargo Airlines along with Shanghai Airlines Cargo. *(Nik French)*

June 26ᵗʰ 2007. In the month that Manchester's runways were re-designated from 06/24 to 05/23 due to the earth's magnetic shift, Royal Thai Air Force B.737-4448 HS-HRH arrived on official visit from Stockholm. *(Nik French)*

July 2ⁿᵈ 2007. Atran Cargo Antonov AN-12 RA-93913 operated a freight charter from/to Moscow-Domodedovo. Visits by this veteran Russian type have continued throughout the 2000s, but this was the only visit of the type during 2007. *(Nik French)*

July 18th 2007. The early-mid 2000s were a great period of growth for Manchester, with many new routes and new airlines starting up. One such airline was Iranian airline Mahan Air, who began a twice-weekly service to Tehran on December 7th 2005. The service was eventually increased to five-weekly in July 2007, but three days after this shot of Airbus A.310 EP-MHE was taken, all flights were suspended following the government's decision to withdraw their operating permit. *(Nik French)*

July 19th 2007. Airbus A.300-622R 5A-DLY. Airbus A.300s were occasional visitors on the airline's Tripoli service, introduced in June 2006 but were suspended in February 2011 due to civil unrest. The service began again in September 2012 with leased Airbus A.320 aircraft. *(Nik French)*

July 30ʰ 2007. Guatemalan-registered Douglas DC-9-51 TG-JII staged through Manchester on delivery to Dubai-based airline Eastern Skyjets and eventually becoming A6-ESA. *(Nik French)*

October 7ʰ 2007. Air China possibly surprised everyone by commencing a three-times-weekly freight service in September 2007. Flight CAO1046/7 would serve Shanghai via Copenhagen three-times weekly, lasting until May 2009. *(Nik French)*

October 16th 2007. Aeroflot Cargo Douglas DC-10 VP-BDG. This was a phenomenal year for freight at Manchester. Aeroflot had started two weeks earlier with a once-weekly flight to Moscow via Frankfurt-Hahn and the following roll-call of cargo airlines serving Manchester by this time were highly impressive: Air China three-weekly, Cathay Pacific thirteen-weekly, China Airlines three-weekly, FedEx four-weekly, Great Wall four-weekly and Jett8 Cargo two-weekly. *(Nik French)*

October 1st 2007. Air Asia Airbus A.320 9M-AFC arrived on a promotional visit on behalf of Manchester United, similar to its previous visit in June 2006. It arrived from Kuala Lumpur via Karachi and Larnaca, stayed for three days during which time it operated a local flight. *(Nik French)*

December 22ⁿᵈ 2007. Cathay Pacific Cargo B.747-467BCF B-HKS. Despite ceasing passenger operations in July 2001 after twelve years, freight operations continue into 2013, having initially taken over the cargo operations of Dragonair in July 2002. *(Nik French)*

January 14ᵗʰ 2008. Today was interesting as Heathrow had been suffering from dense fog until tea-time. In days gone by Manchester would have probably received a bumper crop of diversions, but modern technology precludes such occasions nowadays. However, we did receive one such diversion in the form of brand-new Kenya Airways Boeing 737-800 5Y-KYE. It was on delivery from Boeing Field and due to be delivered through Heathrow, but after a considerable time holding it made its way to Manchester. *(Nik French)*

February 19th 2008. An unusual military visitor to Manchester was Army Air Corps Lynx AH.7 XZ609, which diverted in for fuel. Another diversion visible in the background is Beluga F-GSTD/4 due to fog at Hawarden. *(Nik French)*

May 14th 2008. Atlant Soyuz Tupolev TU-154M RA-85740, another Atlant example RA-85709 and Rossiya Aviation RA-85659 all made rare appearances at Manchester in connection with the UEFA Cup Final between Zenit St.Petersburg and Scottish side Rangers, taking place at the Eastlands Stadium, Manchester. All three TU-154 aircraft were making their last visits to Manchester. *(Geoff Ball)*

May 14ᵗʰ 2008. The match itself provided the customary deluge of executive visitors from all over Europe. One of the more colourful ones to visit on this glorious day was this Jetflite Canadair CL.604 Challenger OH-WIC, which arrived from Moscow-Vnukovo. *(Michael Oldham)*

May 14ᵗʰ 2008. FedEx had made several visits to Manchester by the time they began a four-times-weekly feeder service to Stansted in June 1999. This continued until they introduced a four-times-weekly flight between Paris CDG-Manchester-Memphis, with the first flight being operated by MD-11 N523FE, but sadly it only lasted until August 27ᵗʰ the following year. In 2013 the airline operates to Paris via Birmingham and a link with Stansted continues, currently with ATR-42s. On a hectic day with lots of extra football traffic, MD-11 N597FE is seen on a gloriously sunny evening rolling to a stop on Runway 05L. *(Rick Ward)*

May 14ᵗʰ 2008. Two more aircraft from the day of the final are bringing in Russian football fans. Yakolev Yak-42 Centre-Avia RA-42385 pictured above, which arrived from St. Petersburg, was the last Yak-42 to visit Manchester. Twelve different aircraft visited between 1992 and 2008, with the first being Aeroflot CCCP42544 on April 11ᵗʰ 1992. The shot below was the first Transaero aircraft to visit Manchester, although Boeing 747-219B VP-BQC had visited several times before operating for Virgin Atlantic as G-VPUF. *(Above Geoff Ball, below Michael Oldham)*

July 12ʰ 2008. This dramatic shot was taken the day the Super Jumbo made its first appearance at Manchester. The Airbus A.380, the world's largest passenger aircraft performed an overshoot at 1324 having previously performed a flyover at Goodwood races. A.380-841 F-WWDD then proceeded to Liverpool for a further overshoot. It would be a further fifteen months before the first one would actually land! *(Nik French)*

October 25ʰ 2008. Boeing 747-4HA OO-THA was on a mission of mercy when it arrived as UAE9973 from Dubai. It was carrying a replacement engine for Emirates Boeing 777-31HER A6-EBX which arrived with an engine problem whilst operating UAE017 two days earlier. *(Nik French)*

January 5th 2009. Saudia Boeing 777-268 HZ-AKG. In 2007, the airline added to the growing number of Middle Eastern carriers serving Manchester when, on June 22nd 2007, this very same aircraft operated the first of a twice-weekly scheduled service to Jeddah and Riyadh via Geneva. Unfortunately, this was another service destined not to last as it ceased in December 2009. *(Geoff Ball)*

May 4th 2009. Libyan Air Cargo Antonov AN-124 5A-DKN made an impressive three visits during the month. Each time it arrived to transport a cargo of fuel trucks out to Chad on behalf of the United Nations. *(Nik French)*

September 1st 2009. From humble beginnings back in November 1990 when they began a twice-weekly Airbus A.310 service to Dubai via Frankfurt, Emirates was now operating a double-daily service to Dubai, up to this point with Boeing 777-300ERs. However, today was the day the Airbus A.380 was introduced to the morning (UAE017/8) flight. A6-EDL was use on the inaugural flight amidst much fanfare which saw thousands of extra visitors to the Viewing Park and various other locations around the airport. *(Nik French)*

February 19th 2010. Air Transport International Douglas DC-8-71F N830BX proved to be the penultimate visit of a Douglas DC-8 to Manchester, but the reason for its final appearance was very unusual to say the least! It had been chartered by a wealthy lady who was moving from Kansas City back to the UK and she used the DC-8 (which started life as N8083U with United Airlines) as her removal van! *(Nik French)*

November 4th 2010. Alwafeer Air Boeing 747- 4H6 HZ-AW3 operating a rare Hadj flight. These pilgrimage flights were commonplace in the mid-late 1990s when airlines such as Egyptair, Saudia, Royal Jordanian and Sudan Airways would operate extra flights. Nowadays with the wide choice of direct flights to the Middle East from Manchester by Emirates, Etihad and Qatar Airways, these flights are almost a thing of the past. *(Geoff Ball)*

November 11th 2010. The first Boeing C-17 Globemaster to visit Manchester took place on December 12th 2002, when RAF example ZZ172 diverted in due to bad weather at Brize Norton. A7-MAB is one of two Globemasters operated by the Qatar Emiri Air Force, which make occasional rest stops for the crew whilst en route from Qatar to the United States or vice-versa. *(Nik French)*

December 18th 2010. Malaysia Maritime Defence Force Canadair CL-415 M71-01 arrived amidst a wintry period of weather. It's seen here prior to its long flight back to back to Malaysia after maintenance in Canada. This was the aircraft's second visit, having been originally delivered through Manchester in November 2008 as C-FTBZ. *(Geoff Ball)*

January 11th 2011. This very arty shot shows RAF VC-10 C.1K XV108 about to depart back to Brize Norton, having arrived from an unspecified destination. *(Nik French)*

February 22nd 2011. Cessna Citation Mustang G-FBKD is seen wearing its very smart 'Lotus Cars' colours and logo. This corporate jet is owned by Blink Ltd, a company based at Blackbushe who operate several Mustangs and specialize in low-cost corporate jet charters. *(Geoff Ball)*

April 7th 2011. Battle of Britain Memorial Flight Douglas DC-3 ZA947 arrived at Manchester on March 24th 2011 for a paint job with Air Livery. It was rolled out of the hangar on April 5th in new colours, but absolutely resplendent. It was due to leave two days later but had technical issues and spent a further few days, this time in the Thomas Cook hangar before finally leaving for RAF Coningsby on April 11th. *(Geoff Ball)*

June 14ᵗʰ 2011. This shot shows the only appearance so far, albeit on overshoot as they did not land, of the RAF's latest fighter, the Typhoon. These two aircraft, FGA.4 ZJ941/QO-J & FG.2 ZJ942/DD appeared unexpectedly on the ILS and overshot in formation at 1633. *(Geoff Ball)*

September 29ᵗʰ 2011. Astraeus Boeing 757-2Q8 G-STRX was repainted in this special "Iron Maiden" colour scheme for the "The Final Frontier World Tour 2011" in February 2011 and was operating for Jet2 during the day. When he wasn't performing, the lead singer of Iron Maiden, Bruce Dickinson, was an Astraeus Captain flying the Boeing 757, but unfortunately the airline folded in November 2011. *(Nik French)*

February 6th 2012. The theme of Russian built-aircraft disappearing from Manchester continues with this aircraft, which has proved so far to be the final Ilyushin IL-76 to visit. This flight had diverted to Prestwick the previous evening due to fog at Manchester, but waited at Prestwick for an improvement in the weather. Its outbound cargo needed to be loaded by specialist crane, which had been specially ordered and was waiting to do the job! *(Geoff Ball)*

March 26th 2012. Etihad, who now operate a double daily service to Abu Dhabi, used the very colourful and larger Airbus A.330-300 A6-AFA on this occasion. It's seen wearing special colours 'Visit Abu Dhabi 2012' about to touch down on Runway 23LR operating ETH021. *(Geoff Ball)*

September 19th 2012. In March 2012, Hong Kong Airlines began a business-class only service between London Gatwick and Hong Kong which proved to be a disaster. The flights only lasted six months and had ceased by the time this picture of A.330-243 B-LNL was taken. It arrived to take Manchester City FC out to Madrid for the first round of the 2012/13 Champions League. *(Nik French)*

April 24th 2012. The shape of things to come! The first and only Boeing 787 to visit so far, representing the technological future of the Boeing Corporation. The first Boeing 787s to operate from Manchester should be those of Thomson Airways, possibly by July 2013, although the introduction has been much delayed due to teething troubles. *(Geoff Ball)*

July 30ᵗʰ 2012. Ex-Alitalia Boeing 767-31B EI-CRF arrived on July 18ᵗʰ to become D-ABUM with Condor. It was towed out of the Air Livery hangar on this date in the very smart Condor retro scheme. *(Geoff Ball)*

October 21ˢᵗ 2012. The last Aerospatiale Guppy to visit Manchester in connection with the transportation of Airbus wings was F-GEAI on July 10ᵗʰ 1996. All four Guppy aircraft were withdrawn soon afterwards and from then, all Airbus flights operated direct from Hawarden with their new Airbus A.300-600ST Belugas. Since then, the only Beluga visits to Manchester would be due to bad weather to Hawarden. This visit of F-GSTB/2 was one such occasion. *(Geoff Ball)*

March 19th 2012 (above) and February 28th 2013 (below).

Two contrasting views less than twelve months apart show the massive feat of workmanship. Work on the 60-metre tall (197ft) shaft of Manchester Airport's new Air Traffic Control (ATC) began on Tuesday March 13th 2012 when for 222 consecutive hours until Thursday March 22nd, concrete was continuously poured to help create the base. This method of pouring concrete into a continuously moving form is known as 'slipform' and is the same construction technique that was used to construct the famous CN Tower in Toronto, officially recognised as the tallest building in the world from 1976 to 2007. Teams of twenty construction operatives worked 24 hours a day on an elevated hydraulic platform surrounding shaft, inserting steel reinforcing rods into the concrete and 'polishing' the shaft as it grew, to ensure a smooth finish to the structure. Around 600 cubic metres (m3) of concrete and 65 tons of steel reinforcement were cast to form the nine-metre wide shaft of the

new ATC tower. It took one of the tallest cranes in Europe to put the finishing touches to the structure of Manchester Airport's newly constructed £16 million Air Traffic Control Tower. The crane was needed to lift the 168 tonne sub-cab section up 60 metres in the air, before being guided to its finished position on the top of the tower shaft, to give the tower its finished effect on the Manchester skyline. The sub-cab is the equivalent size of a four-storey detached house and has been built on the ground before being hoisted up by the super crane and permanently placed on top of the newly built tower shaft. It took six smaller cranes to assemble the finished 90 metre tall crane in order to enable it to carry out the works. The crane was brought in on 25 articulated lorries to the site. The super crane lifted the sub-cab onto the column, with two 'banksmen' sitting on top with radios, charged with guiding the two 10mm guide rods into place. The sub-cab will home several departments including fire watch and apron control who guide aircraft to their gates. (Both photos Geoff Ball)

117

May 19th 2013. These shots show the first Boeing 787 to operate a commercial service from Manchester, bringing the airport's story right up to date. The type had been grounded worldwide on January 16th due to several problems, including issues with the battery system which could be prone to overheating or catching fire. This grounding was rescinded on April 27th and only three days prior to this photo, Qatar Airways announced that they would be operating a Boeing 787 Dreamliner on the morning QTR041/2 flight. A7-BCC is seen early on this misty Sunday morning on short finals to Runway 05L. *(Above Nik French, below Geoff Ball)*

May 2013. Panoramic view of the airport, as seen by the controllers from the tower. *(Nik French)*

May 2013. The tower lit up at night. *(Nik French)*

INTERNATIONAL AIRLINES 1938-2013

The following is a listing of all the International airlines that have operated scheduled or charter flights through Manchester, together with the start date and the aircraft operating the initial flight.

Country	Airline	First Flight	Operated By
AP- (Pakistan)	Air Blue	1 June 2007	A.321 AP-BJA
	PIA	28 March 1989	B.747 AP-BCO
A4O- (Bahrain)	Gulf Air	25 October 1992	B.763 A4O-GG
A6- (UAE)	Emirates	2 November 1990	A.310 A6-EKA
	Etihad	26 March 2006	A.332 A6-EYE
A7- (Qatar)	Qatar Airways	2 April 2003	A.300 A7-ABX
B- (China)	Air China Cargo	1 September 2007	B.747F B-2409
	Cathay Pacific	1 July 2002 (CARGO)	B.747F B-HME
	China Airlines	2 May 2002	B.747F B-18755
	Dragonair	29 July 2000	B.747F N507MC
	Great Wall	3 May 2007	B.747F B-2429
CF- (Canada)	Air Canada	25 May 1965 (Charter)	DC8 CF-TJP
	Air Canada	28 April 1986 (Scheduled)	B.747 C-FTOE
	Air Transat	23 July 1989	L.1011 C-FTNC
	Canada 3000	25 May 1989	B.757 C-FOOE
	Canadian	02 January 1990	A.310 C-GJWD
	Club Air	24 June 1994	B.747 C-GCIH
	CP Air	24 May 1975	DC8 CF-CPT
	HMY Airlines	17 December 2002	B.757 C-GMYD
	Nationair	2 July 1985	DC8 C-GMXR
	Ontario World	7 May 1979	B.707 C-GRYN
	Ports Of Call	23 May 1989	DC8 C-FNZE
	Quebecair	6 May 1985	DC8 C-GQBA
	Royal Airlines	22 May 1995	L.1011 C-FTNI
	Skyservices	18 May 2005	B.757 C-GMYH
	Wardair	6 June 1969	B.707 CF-ZYP
	Zoom	29 June 2003	B.763 C-GZUM
CCCP- (Soviet Union)	Aeroflot	29 June 1980 (Charter)	Tu-134 65770
	Aeroflot	26 July 1987 (Scheduled)	Tu-154 85592
	Aeroflot Cargo	2 October 2007	DC10 VP-BDE
CN- (Morocco)	Royal Air Maroc	12 July 1982	B.727 CN-CCH

CS- (Portugal)	Air Atlantis	3 May 1988	B.727 CS-TBK
	Air Columbus	1 November 1989	B.727 CS-TKA
	Air Portugal	12 May 1981	B.727 CS-TBL
	Portugalia	19 May 1997	Fk-100 CS-TPE
	SATA	3 May 2008	A.320 CS-TKK
	Sul Air	3 January 1991	B.737 CS-TMC
	TAP	31 May 1965	L-1049 CS-TLA
CU- (Cuba)	Cubana	19 December 1997	DC10 F-GTDF
D- (Germany)	Aero Lloyd	23 May 2001	A.321 D-ALAK
	Air Berlin	1 November 2004	B.738 D-ABAN
	Bavaria	27 May 1967	Herald D-BEBE
	Condor	31 May 1964	Viscount D-ANOL
	Germania	7 May 2013	A.319 D-ASTY
	Germanwings	25 October 2009	A.319 D-AGWK
	Hamburg Intl	11 February 2006	B.73G D-AHIC
	HLX Express	31 March 2003	B.73G D-AGEU
	LTS	20 December 1986	B.757 D-AMUT
	Lufthansa	23 April 1956	L-1649 D-ALIN
	Lufthansa Cargo	1 November 2009	MD11 D-ALCA
	NFD	21 April 1987	Metro D-CABE
	OLT	18 November 1999	Saab 340 D-COLE
	WDL	29 June 1981	F.27 D-BAKA
EC- (Spain)	Aebul	6 August 2000	B.717 EC-HNY
	Air Class	25 May 2006	B.737 EC-JSL
	Air Europa	8 November 1987	B.733 EC-ECM
	Air Nostrum	1 February 2004	CRJ EC-GYI
	Air Spain	13 May 1972	DC8 EC-BZQ
	Aviaco	5 June 1960	CV-440 EC-APV
	Canafrica	5 May 1989	MD83 EC-ECO
	Centennial	22 May 1993	MD83 EC-389
	Futura	17 February 1990	B.734 EC-401
	Hola Airlines	5 May 2002	B.734 EC-GNZ
	Hispania	28 May 1983	SE.210 EC-CIZ
	Iberia	30 June 1964 (Charter)	L-1049 EC-AMQ
	Iberia	28 March 1982 (Scheduled)	DC9 EC-BPG
	Iberworld	1 May 1999	A.320 EC-GUR

	L.A.Canarias	5 May 1989	MD83 EC-EMG
	LTE	23 May 1992	B.757 EC-EGH
	Nortjet	27 May 1989	B.734 EC-EMI
	Oasis	27 May 1989	MD83 EC-269
	Spanair	19 May1989	MD83 EC-EJU
	Spantax	12 May 1963	DC7 EC-ATR
	South Atlantic AL	13 May 2001	B.757 EC-HUT
	Swiftair	15 November 2004	ATR-72 EC-IYH
	TAE	6 May 1979	SE.210 EC-CMS
	Trans Europa	19 May 1967	DC7 EC-BCH
	Universair	5 September 1987	B.733 EC-EDM
	Viva	11 August 1989	B.733 EC-EII
EI- (Republic of Ireland)	Aer Arran	9 June 2003	ATR-42 EI-CVS
	Aer Lingus	1 July 1947	DC3 EI-ACT
	Air Contractors	3 November 2003	BAe.748 G-ORAL
	Clyden Airways	17 September 1978	DC3 EI-BDT
	EU Jet	4 October 2004	Fk-100 EI-DFC
	Ryanair	1 June 1987	BAC 1-11 EI-BSY
	Translift	27 June 1992	DC8 EI-TLD
EP- (Iran)	Mahan Air	4 January 2006	A.310 F-OJHI
ES- (Estonia)	Estonian Air	10 May 2005	B.735 ES-ABI
EW- (Belarus)	Belavia	5 June 2005	B.735 EW-251PA
EZ- (Turkmenistan)	Turkmenistan AL	7 December 2001	B.757 EZ-A014
F- (France)	Air France	16 June 1946	DC3 F-BAXD
	Air Littoral	09 April 1990	EMB-120 F-GFER
	Air Toulouse	27 December 1993	B.734 F-GFUH
	Regional Airlines	28 March 1994	Jetstream F-GMVN
	TAT	27 March 1994	F.28 F-BUTI
	UAT	31 May 1963	DC6 F-BGSL
IIA- (Hungary)	Malev	1 July 2001	Fk-70 HA-LMF
HB- (Switzerland)	Air Engiadina	1 April 1997	Do.328 HB-AEI
	Balair	24 June 1960	Viking HB-AAR
	Crossair	30 October 1995	Saab 2000 HB-IZF
	Fly Hello	2 May 2005	MD90 HB-JIB
	Globe Air	22 May 1965	Herald HB-AAK
	Phoenix Aviation	26 May 1972	B.707 N732TW

	Swissair	12 December 1948	DC3 HB-IRN
HZ- (Saudia Arabia)	Saudia	22 June 2007	B.777 HZ-AKG
I- (Italy)	Alitalia	1 August 2004	Emb-170 EI-DFJ
	ATI	21 May 1985	DC9 I-ATIJ
	Azzura Air	27 October 2001	B.73G D-AGEY
	Itavia	2 June 1963	Herald I-TIVE
	SAM	1 June 1963	DC6 I-DIMU
	Volare	28 October 2007	A.320 I-WEBB
LN- (Norway)	Braathens	26 May 1963	F.27 LN-SUO
	Malmo Aviation	2 June 2001	BAE.146 SE-DSS
	Nor-Fly	2 May 1981	CV-580 LN-BWG
	Norwegian Shuttle	6 April 2006	B.733 LN-KKJ
	Wideroe	1 December 2003	Dash-8 LN-WDC
LX- (Luxembourg)	Cargolux	19 August 1996	B.747F N809MC
	Luxair	14 May 1966 (Charter)	Viscount LX-LGC
	Luxair	27 March 1995 (Scheduled)	Emb-120 LX-LGL
LY- (Lithuania)	Aurela	1 June 2012	B.733 LY-SKA
LZ- (Bulgaria)	Balkan	18 May 1968	IL-18 LZ-BET
	Balkan Holidays	2 February 2002	Tu-154 LZ-HMI
	Bulgaria Air	2 October 2005	B.735 LZ-BOR
	Hemus Air	3 March 2001	Tu-154 LZ-HMS
	VIA Air	7 May 1995	Tu-154 LZ-MIR
N (USA)	Air America	3 August 1989	L.1011 N303EA
	Air Express Intl	12 December 1982	CL-44 N121AE
	Air Florida	11 May 1980	DC10 N1035F
	American Airlines	1 May 1986	B.767 N319AA
	American Transair	16 June 1989	L.1011 N190AT
	Continental	20 May 1995	B.757 N12114
	Delta	27 June 1991	B.763 N176DN
	Emery Worldwide	15 May 1985	DC8 N2674U
	FedEx	28 August 2007	MD11 N523FE
	Polar Cargo	17 April 1997	B.747F N920FT
	Rich International	1 May 1994	L.1011 N300AW
	TIA	6 May 1979	DC-10 N103TV
	TWA	28 May 1978	B.707 N18712
	Northwest Orient	12 September 1979	B.747F N616US

	Southern Intl	16 May 1992	DC8F N871SJ
	US Air	26 May 2000	B.767 N655US
	World Airways	31 March 1978	DC10 N103WA
OE- (Austria)	Austrian Airlines	23 May 1965 (Charter)	Viscount OE-LAH
	Austrian Airlines	3 April 1980 (Scheduled)	DC9 OE-LDB
	Inter-Sky	21 December 2002	Dash-8 OE-LSB
	Lauda Air	19 December 1992 (Charter)	B.733 OE-ILF
	Lauda Air	8 April 1994 (Scheduled)	CRJ OE-LRB
	Rheintalflug	8 April 2002	Emb-145 OE-LSM
	Tyrolean Airways	27 May 2000	Fk-100 OE-LFK
OH- (Finland)	Finnair	1 April 1977 (Cargo)	DC6 OH-KDA
	Finnair	27 March 1994 (Passenger)	MD80 OH-LMA
OK-(Czechoslovakia)	CSA	13 June 1992	Tu-134 OK-EFK
	Danube Wings	6 January 2010	B.734 OK-WGY
OM- (Slovakia)	Sky Europe	9 April 2005	B.733 OM-SED
OO- (Belgium)	DHL	7 January 1992	CV-580 OO-DHG
	Sabena	15 June 1949	DC3 OO-AUV
	SN Brussels AL	19 November 2001	RJ-100 OO-DWK
	TEA	5 June1978	B.707 OO-TED
	VLM	21 September 1998	Fk-50 OO-VLK
OY- (Denmark)	Maersk	1 November 2004	B.735 OY-API
	Newair	28 October 1991	Jetstream OY-CRR
	Sterling	7 July 1965	DC6 OY-BAS
	Sun-Air	20 January 1997	Do.328 OY-SVW
PH- (Netherlands)	BASE Airlines	6 December 1990	Jetstream PH-KJA
	Dutchbird	29 January 2004	A.320 PH-VAC
	KLM	24 June 1938	DC2 PH-AKP
	Schreiner AW	11 May 1965	F.27 PH-SAD
SE- (Sweden)	Air Ops	7 May 1994	L.1011 SE-DPX
	City Airlines	10 September 2001	EMB-135 SE-RAB
	SAS	1 April 1966	SE.210 SE-DAC
	Skyways	31 October 1999	Emb-145 SE-DZD
	Transair	10 May 1962	DC6 SE-BDI
	Transjet	25 May 2001	MD83 SE-RBI
	Transwede	30 April 1995	MD87 SE-DHG
	Viking Airlines	23 July 2004	MD83 SE-RDF

	West Air Sweden	1 September 2004	ATP SE-LGV
SP- (Poland)	Centralwings	28 October 2007	B.733 SP-LMD
	LOT	5 July 1976 (Charter)	IL-18 SP-LSH
	LOT	1 June 1980 (Scheduled)	Tu-134 SP-LHD
SU- (Egypt)	Air Luxor	17 February 2001	A.320 CS-TNE
	Egyptair	15 July 1994	A.320 SU-GBC
SX- (Greece)	Aegean Airways	7 May 2004	B.734 SX-BGR
	Alexandair	14 May 2005	MD83 SX-BMP
	Axon Airlines	15 May 2001	B.73G SX-BLT
	Electra Airlines	27 June 2002	DC10 SX-CVP
	Galaxy Airlines	23 May 2000	B.734 SX-BFA
	Hellas Jet	3 May 2004	A.320 SX-BVC
	Olympic	22 June 2000	B.733 SX-BLA
	Bangladesh Biman	8 April 2006	DC10 S2-ACS
S7- (Seychelles)	Air Seychelles	20 January 1996	B.767 S7-AAS
TC- (Turkey)	Alfa Air	20 July 1998	A.300 TC-ALR
	Atlas Jet Intl	1 August 2005	B.757 TC-OGG
	Euro Sun	11 September 2000	B.737 TC-ESB
	Freebird Airlines	27 December 2003	A.321 TC-FBT
	Istanbul Airlines	16 April 1992	B.734 TC-ACA
	KTHY	31 March 2001	B.738 TC-MSO
	Onur Air	4 May 1995	A.320 TC-ONA
	Pegasus	30 May 1994	MD80 N500TR
	Saga Airlines	9 May 2009	B.738 SE-RHR
	Sky Airlines	4 June 2010	A.321 TC-SKI
	Sunways	9 April 1995	MD80 TC-INB
	THY	2 June 1993	B.735 TC-JDV
	Top Air	6 June 1997	B.727 TC-IYA
	Turkuaz Airlines	3 July 2009	A.321 TC-TCE
TF- (Iceland)	Air Atlanta	13 July 1995	B.747 TF-ABW
	Icelandair	30 June 1997	B.734 TF-FIB
	Islandflug	7 April 2001	B.733 TF-FDA
	MD Airlines	3 July 2002	MD83 TF-MDD
TS- (Tunisia)	Karthago Airlines	24 May 2008	B.733 TS-IED
	Nouvelair	24 May 1991	MD80 F-GHED
	Tunis Air	3 May 1983 (Charter)	B.737 TS-IOD

	Tunis Air	21 May 2011 (Scheduled)	A.320 TS-IMG
UK- (Uzbekistan)	Uzbekistan Airlines	17 November 1994	IL-62 UK-86577
UR- (Ukraine)	Air Ukraine	10 April 1993	Yak-42 UR-42544
VH- (Australia)	Qantas	1 April 1983	B.747 VH-EBM
VR-H (Hong Kong)	Air Hong Kong	20 October 1989	B.707F VR-HKL
	Cathay Pacific	31 October 1989	B.747 VR-HOO
VT- (India)	Air India	17 November 1995	A.310 VT-EJG
YK- (Syria)	Syrianair	14 June 2004	A.320 YK-AKC
YL- (Latvia)	Air Baltic	16 July 2004	B.734 YL-BAK
	Latvian Charter	1 July 1995	Yak-42 RA-42428
YR- (Romania)	Tarom	15 May 1971 (Charter)	IL-18 YR-IML
	Tarom	28 March 1994 (Scheduled)	BAC 1-11 YR-BCK
YU- (Yugoslavia)	Aviogenex	4 May 1969	Tu-134 YU-AHH
	Inex-Adria	26 May 1963	DC6 YU-AFE
	JAT	5 May 1968	SE.210 YU-AHF
ZS- (South Africa)	South African	27 March 1990	B.747 ZS-SAP
3B- (Mauritius)	Air Mauritius	11 April 1996	A.340 3B-NAT
4K- (Azerbaijan)	Azerbaijan AL	18 July 2002	B.757 4K-AZ12
4X- (Israel)	EL AL	21 October 1980	B.747 4X-AXF
5A- (Libya)	Libyan Arab	18 June 2006	A.320 TS-INJ
5B- (Cyprus)	Cyprus Airways	6 April 1973	Trident 2 5B-DAC
	Eurocypria	27 March 1992	A.320 5B-DBC
	Helios Airways	26 July 2000	B.734 5B-DBG
6Y- (Jamaica)	Air Jamaica	1 June 2002	A.340 6Y-JMM
7T- (Algeria)	Air Algerie	18 December 2002	B.73G 7T-VJS
9A- (Croatia)	Croatian Airlines	18 May 1991	MD80 YU-ANO
	Dubrovnik Airlines	27 May 2008	MD83 9A-CDB
9H- (Malta)	Air Malta	7 April 1974	B.720 AP-AMG
9M- (Malaysia)	Malaysian Airlines	30 March 1999	B.777 9M-MRF
	MAS Kargo	3 April 2004	B.747F TF-ARN
	Jett8 Cargo	4 July 2007	B.747F 9V-JEA
9V- (Singapore)	Singapore Airlines	3 April 1986	B.743 9V-SKM
9Y- (West Indies)	BWIA	14 July 2002	L.1011 9Y-THA